For Understanding Eyes

Charles Holmes

For Understanding Eyes

Copyright © 2019 Charles Holmes

Printed in the United States of America

Published by

Big Hat Press
Lafayette, California
www.bighatpress.com

Cover Painting | 19th Century Art
"Red Roses"
A Gift of Lizzy Neidhoefier

DEDICATED TO

Rosalie Louise Gallick, my mother, who enjoyed quiet churches, entertaining community gatherings (radio too) with piano and song, and fulfilling her lifelong ministry of goodness.

Charles John Holmes Sr., my father, a skilled craftsman with hand and pen, who loved the sea, stamp collecting, and baseball.

Aidan Lee Elenteny, my surrogate grandson. May he strive wisely to become the best possible person, and look at the years with understanding eyes and a loving heart!

BOOKS BY CHARLES HOLMES

ADULT BOOKS

Streets That Speak*
For Understanding Eyes
Reflections of the Heart
Reflections of the Soul
Thoughts From Millie**

*About streets that do not have enough and streets that do have enough

**Interview quotes/practical wisdom from an elder at 89, 90, and 91 years old

CHILDREN'S BOOKS

Kid-like Poetry with a Bit of a Smile...Sometimes
Kid-like Poetry for Kids Who Are "Cool" at School
Kid-like Poetry for Kids Who Like Recess
Bo Loney Goes to a New School
The Silver-lettered Poem in the Sky
The Cloth of 100 Wrinkles
Aidan Dreams Amazing Dreams
Aidan Dreams of 105 Fortune Cookies

Available on Amazon

CONTENTS

I
Shades of Green

II
Shades of Blue

III
Shades of Brown

For Understanding Eyes

I
Shades of Green

To Accept What Is

One of the hardest inner challenges:
to accept everything
that is happening to us,
a power that dulls discord,
calms precious hours,
blesses human days.
An unspeakable triumph,
and yet,
to be awake, alert, wise,
focus on own self-care,
put less weight on stress that tenses,
use today's time well.

Appreciation

To appreciate being alive,
    be attentive in the day,
take meaningful steps
    with a "cool head"
and becoming spirit,
    which summons the heart
to awaken wisely,
    not worrying about noise that comes,
if darkness looms,
    take some deep breaths
and expect to create today's hope.

"They"

If your thinking is different, "they" don't like you.

If you're highly educated and they're not,
"they" don't like you.

If you can do what they can't,
and would like to do, "they" don't like you.

If you have less money, no social success
nor substantial accomplishment, they forget you.

If you win the lottery and become famous,
"they" remember you and like you.

Common Sayings

Everything has a purpose.
  "Not always."
What goes around, comes around.
  "Not always."
Find the nugget in the situation.
  "Not always."
Every cloud has a silver lining.
  "Not always."
Blessing in disguise.
  "Not always."
Take with a grain of salt.
  "Not always."
We all make mistakes.
  "They got that right."

Surrogate Grandfather

To help lift a child to full maturity,
have a deep feeling of that possibility!
Will my hopeful vision ever lessen?
Will I find a sensible way through sudden shadows?
Will my energy withstand time's cruelty?
Why not a concrete miracle,
like the sea, sky, stone, flower, tree…?
What a blessing to be heartfelt support,
a weathered elder
contributing a grand, connected fragment
to a wonderful, living soul!

Attempted Spirituality

He took the "road less traveled"
        that led to childish naivety,
making some sad decisions.

Ascetic living is a way,
        but can go too far,
as he knows so well.

The trail of poverty has a solid,
        spiritual place, provided
steps have wisdom and vision.

Abstinence also has a corner,
        but needs balanced love
and continual meditation to see rich fulfillment.

If sufficient emotional support is lacking,
        spirituality can emerge, but also
emptiness and aloneness.

Some look back at the "road,"
        feel its bumps and plodding ways,
and find rounded, polished pebbles.

Still, more than a few forget,
        every soul
is responsible for the time given.

How Many?

How many shore rocks enjoy splashing water?
    Winding rivers wonder where they are going?
    Still forests whisper to their well-worn trails?
    Speaking oceans are multi-lingual?

How many take dawn's light and fresh spirit for granted?
    Try to sense the feelings of a tree?
    Gaze with spontaneous joy at shifting autumn leaves?
    Smile calmly at the magic of silent rain?

How many deeply care about the broken-hearted?
    Take in the feeling of elders who wonder will they have enough?
    Remember two memorable words from those who went through
    the Great Depression, "Don't waste!"?

One Way to Glance

The poet Emily Dickinson writes
  "I dwell in possibility." *
Einstein says
  "Imagination is more important
than knowledge." **
  Nietzsche notes
"He who has a why to live
  can bear almost any how." ***
Thoreau states "Thought is the sculptor
  who can create the person you want to be." ****
Intelligible conclusion:
  it's the way you look at things;
imagine possibilities.

Emily Dickinson 1830-1886
**Albert Einstein 1879-1955*
***Friedrich Nietzsche 1844-1900*
****Henry David Thoreau 1817-1862*

A Stone

Does absurdity give birth to a dancing stone,
        which the sun finds smooth and shiny?
Its spirit is great
        because it's close to the earth,
stranger to ears
        but not to feet.
Though hard by nature,
        is there a tender core,
a caring soul?

Nurturing

It's an art to nurture self,
but why does it take so long?

I tried to do it by myself,
another mistake with the others.

It was born when I held
a 3 day old baby in my arms.

He gave me a poetic voice;
before it was idealistic prose.

He launched waves of delight,
meaning for my soul.

He presented gentle grace, a spirit gift,
spiritual map for dancing feet.

He provided many little joys,
which were in reality big joys.

Purpose came to an elder.
He needed me and I needed him.

Individual Needs

We all need someone
　　to talk to,
　　think about,
　　love…and be loved.
If these joys not alive in a life,
　　the heart feels
　　clinging sadness,
　　the soul watches
　　time wither, tomorrow's
　　moonlight dance
　　a little closer.

Smattering

Incompetence reigns,
    doesn't bother the squirrel,
there's always a road
    and a tree.

What I See

The quality of my soul matters most,
     a spirit who did not strive for power,
but somehow to give honor to the day,
     reverence in one's stay.
Have I had a spiritual experience?
     What is a spiritual experience?
Do I know what it means
     to be fully human?
I chose to "turn the other cheek" many times.
     Was I right?
Or just another mistake among the many?
     Learning and time
have disclosed the satisfying reality
     of not being a stranger to myself.

Waking Tree

Whispering art,
  there alone, not alone,
unflustered by people,
  present, rich, at peace,
speaks its own language,
  passersby wander near,
says Hello without reply,
  non-judgmental gaze,
listens, does it hear?
  observes, does it see?
accepts where it is,
  no gray leaves,
or any visible concern,
  cool and calm.
Contributes greatly,
  yet how many
Good Mornings and Thank Yous
  has it received?

Tea Pot

Splendor within,
    health vessel,
green over black,
    helps feelings,
soothes evening-tide,
    strong purpose,
aids sense of control,
    nugget with warmth,
smooth pour, not to hurry,
    object of artist brush,
helps a lot, yet given little credit.

In Times of Old

In times of old,
    what was sold
was a $5000 house,
    in a good neighborhood.
In times of old,
    what was sold
was an ice cream cone
    for 5 cents.
In times of old,
    what was sold
was a milkshake
    for 25 cents.
In times of old,
    what was sold
was a banana split
    for 35 cents.
Clearly the "Good Ol' Days,"
    but why not think about
the Good New Days?

A Look at Life

Profound sorrow in every life,
    crying hope, more thankful joys,
like converting a weakness into a strength,
    becoming a friend to oneself,
deepening self-knowledge,
    calming nerves better,
growing in self-control and courtesy,
    believing body and spirit can improve.

Hope for the Artist

To be a struggling artist
    whose pen, brush, lens
can touch human spirits,
    making today's steps
more certain than yesterday's,
    on a path winding, sometimes hidden,
with buried goodness, frustrated effort,
    unseen aloneness, unfortunate confusion,
"nobody to talk to" times,
    unexpected naivety, the shock of the real,
yet deep hunger for life ever present,
    and desire to create sincere art.

Giving

Sea urchin ornament
     left at Thrift Shop door
a short time before opening.
     Will aggressive hands
take it to another place,
     or will a hidden kindness
be twice as good?

The Soul

The soul thirsts for all-pervading beauty.
    Upon feeling its unearthly delicacy,
gains confidence and hope,
    steps in unbroken harmony
with inmost core,
    seeing like never before,
healing gifts, precious time,
    plausible possibilities.

Deep-felt Poem

Flashes of imagination,
    creating heartfelt wordings,
autobiographical art,
    pierced now and again
by needles and thorns,
    which guide a pen
to offer four fine lines
    which read better
than a pleasant novel,
    in a magnificent, shadowy world
that witnesses resilient spirits
    search for significant meaning,
    calm amid discord,
    sureness in what you do,
    peace in who you are,
a poem to focus light
    on the learning
you give to yourself.

Success

To know and accept oneself,
long journey,
work at what you really love,
rich blessing,
share with one you love and accept,
generous depth,
be as free as you can be,
a matter of degree,
maintain peace of mind,
spiritual essence of it all.

For Understanding Eyes

II
Shades of Blue

Perfection

Excellence did get a mention,
    but far more often *perfection*.
Subtle seed frequently planted deep,
    to be a whispering tree,
which, even in winter, feeling not free.
    Simple act, spirit hard to see,
then needless gnawing to significant degree.
    Is it childishly plain to suggest,
"Try to do your best"?

Elder Advice

He gazed at the years
    and "placed experience on the table."
Firstly, don't hate those who have wronged you.
Secondly, leave yesterday behind, and
    focus on what you can control today.
Thirdly, don't mind the rumblings, and believe in
    the power of a positive mental attitude.
Fourthly, live each day as well as you can.
Fifthly, hold dear the little joys
    and the love that touches deep.

Knowing

People tell me who I am,
      but they haven't read the book.
A deeper insight,
      do they know themselves?

Presence

The spirit pushes for presence,
the mind for serenity,
the heart for love.

Demeanor, dignified, composed, calm,
spiritual bearing that conveys understanding,
making it easier for a meeting of souls.

To be present to all that is,
everyone's challenge, no one's reality,
but try we must.

Age

The beauty of getting older
    is that you get to slow down,
pay more attention to actions than words,
    be keenly conscious of the art of walking
and think before talking,
    learn about wise caring
and sensible sharing,
    see many things
in a deeper way.

Questions for a Thinking Spirit

How often have we thought we saw the whole,
to find out it was only a part?
Why is it so hard to stay in the moment?
Why is self-acceptance such a long journey?
How many do not put up with fools wisely?
How many adults don't consider today a sacred gift?
How many realize the power of the practitioner's
goodness in performing his or her profession?
What does a mother's love look like
in a child's soul?

Ocean Beach

What a blessing to take in the ocean
    with its wild, freshening might
and vast, measureless expanse,
    where waves are drawn to shore,
golden beach stretching far,
    whole seashells sighing in the sand,
seaweed with its complicated tangle,
    dim footprints slowly saying goodbye,
another day of subtle art
    saying hello.

Hard Work and Time

Do we understand what we understand?
So much complexity!
How helped by meditation,
hard work, and time?

Do we connect with what we connect?
So much complexity!
How helped by mindfulness,
hard work, and time?

Do we see what we observe?
So much complexity!
How helped by consciousness,
hard work, and time?

Do we hear what we listen to?
So much complexity!
How helped by wholly focusing,
hard work, and time?

Self-talk

Can't change assumptions,
      things around me,
      lost time, why grieve?
Accept discrimination with age,
      it's part of the culture,
      absurdity on many paths.
Move cautiously with restless tide,
      not analyze too much,
      doesn't help.
Enjoy Now,
      be present to those you meet,
      and to what you do,
always mindful that the day
      will never come again.

White Hair

Older, less attention,
        people look for advantages,
when they see none, they walk by
        with mirrored eyes.

If golden dust suddenly on silken shoes,
        they return,
yet what price,
        wouldn't dignified aloneness be better?

So many think they know you,
        but don't, yet
to be grateful for lessons of the seasons,
        and possibilities on the horizon.

Discord Reigns

Discord seems to permeate the planet.
    Does it lessen the human spirit
in its quest for giving?
    How much freedom does it curtail?
How to move to a more calm state of mind?
    "Thinking makes it so." *

* *Shakespeare's <u>Hamlet</u>, Act II, ii*

Some Steps in a Day

Sixteen waking hours
    to do well what we do,
accept where we are,
    ignore larger forces,
be awake, care wisely,
    eye pleasing little things,
do our best according to our lights.

Movement

Children at playground take it for granted;
  those in residential care do not.
Professional athletes display its grace;
  dancers, its delightful art.

And the body can always improve,
  though time does speak,
sometimes with discouraging words;
  yet it has many healing ways.

Wondrous Clouds

Do they worry when they wander,
    with so much separation?
Do they grasp they are bundles of possibilities,
    or just drops of water in the sky?

Do they stare at planet ceiling,
    at times say hello to radiant blue?
Do they look down with amazement`
    and come out with "Oh My!"?

Do they have a healthy independence
    as they lift, hurry, swirl up, vanish?
Do they feel their beauty to earthly eyes,
    realize their reverent art?

Soul Needs

We all need light in the dark,
     hopeful song at height of storm,
children with scooters making our young side smile,
     pets who provide a home with true warmth.

We all need sun, but not too much,
     cool breeze on summer day,
blue sky, snow-white clouds, cleansing rain,
     peak to see, trail to climb.

We all need clear dawn,
     flying feathers landing on smooth stone,
refreshing ripples on water edge,
     morning's hope and joy.

We all need distinctive gifts which enrich,
     spring flowers and the way they make you feel,
bird chirping on sturdy limb,
     firm rock on which to stand to see ahead.

Beggar's Dollar

Young woman on subway
    holds baby with sad sign.
A man responds, gives a dollar.
    The lady to his right says,
"Every day, every day (she comes)."
    Another who is near nods.

    Where will that bill go?
To a store clerk who gives it for change?
    From there,
will it witness a humanitarian flight,
    arriving for a needy soul
at just the right time?

Selfless Generosity 2018 A.D.

Very sick, end in sight.
He continues
to give half his pension
to a destitute family,
rather than go to residential care,
which he knows he needs.

Hopes and Fears

Do our hopes and fears materialize,
      or do they just fill the mind,
envelope the walls,
      slow down advancing steps?

Poverty

The price of poverty spreads wide.
    It goes into intelligence, abilities,
associations, judgments,
        verbal and non-verbal treatment,
as well as lifestyle.

    And some live their whole life
under its umbrella.
    They have a feeling
which others do not carry with them.
    The unsettling question...
Do they have hope?

To Those...

To those I will not meet again,
may stars shine on their night steps,
blink shrewdly as they turn corners,
wander in the sky beauty for their eyes.

Should they recall their dreams,
may they sparkle,
enlighten the now, the tomorrow,
revealing tender good.

If their aloneness runs a little too deep,
may it teach insights in the sun,
shallow feelings subsiding,
every dawn to have morning freshness.

May they sacrifice but not too much,
bodily aches not diminish consistent whole,
self-tutored wisdom guiding,
full humanity composing a life.

Always

There may always be
    some
who sell their souls,
    but
make allowance for them.
    Their circumstance
of mind and heart
    we may never know...
just how they feel
    when time dwindles down.

Searching Questions

What is the smartest, most wonderful decision of my life?

Who is the greatest person I have ever known?

What is the best contribution I have made thus far?

What was the most important day of my life?

What are my three best talents?

What, other than conscience, can I employ to lead me through suffering ?

What three habits will help me most in becoming the best possible person?

For Understanding Eyes

III
Shades of Brown

Deep Love Never Dies

When a beloved ends earth stay,
    the cards from good souls read,
"Sympathy," "Condolences," "Empathy,"
    but the deeper,
penetrating few words are:
    "Continue loving!"
    "Don't stop the dialogue ever!"

Look At...

Look at sky, imagine,
    at horizon, wonder,
    at feelings, consider,
    at self-image, appreciate.

Look at competence, note details,
    at honesty, breathe in,
    at curiosity, dig wisely,
    at dreams, interpret well.

Look at waterways, write a poem,
    at dawn, rejoice,
    at health, be grateful,
    at life, be satisfied.

Nature Thoughts

To love the flower
    which says
"I don't want to be a decoration on a table;
    I wish to be free by the sea."
To love majestic tree,
    meant for you and me,
limbs reaching out
    to some degree.
To love bed of ivy
    in its calm repose,
handles well
    awakening to garden hose.
To love the garden,
    its beauty and peace,
with fond hope
    it will not cease.
Patiently wait for seeds in the ground
    to grow, not take too long,
then rise to earth's table
    where they belong.

Three Journeys

Three paths in the woods,
    One, outward,
        engaged in service,
        right and thoughtful.
    Two, inward,
        looking within at soul that wants to dance.
    Three, forward,
        wise steps open to possibilities,
        never letting shadows take over,
        looking at the sunny side.

"Now"

Refusing to look at yesterday,
        not eye tomorrow unnecessarily,
embracing today,
        even amidst dark clouds,
intermittent thunder, falling rain.

Grateful for soft breathing,
        nurturing self tenderly
with positive mental attitude,
        hope in forming relationships,
work that has considerable meaning.

Always to learn from elders,
        who refuse to rush, extra careful,
slow down,
        do one thing at a time,
picture what they want,
        and go for it.

The Feeling

For those who know the feeling
    of going through most of life
without supporting family,
    of empty, at times discordant, holidays,
of growing up without connecting relatives,
    of thin emotional and financial realities,
of not having a roof to call one's own,
    of expenses far exceeding
pension and social security,
    of being labelled "doesn't have much"
and treated sometimes in a lesser way,

    ENJOY WHAT YOU HAVE.

Great Souls

Evil never sleeps,
        yet there are many great souls
in this beautiful, cruel world
        researchers will never find.

Some, on stage;
        others, in the audience;
still others, on sidewalks
        near and far from theater lights.

They help others,
        challenge self outside of comfort zone,
focus on personal growth,
        and do they feel
they don't owe anyone their story?

If You Want To…

If you want to delve into spirituality,
    explore anthropology.
If you want to express spirituality,
    work on creativity.
If you want to write about life,
    be a poet.
If you want to better your well-being,
    pray for someone or something.
If you want to grow in compassion,
    see, hear, forgive, reach out.
If you want to appreciate truth,
    step into nature, dreams, meditation.
If you want to discover the magic of study,
    study and study and study.
If you want to find one of life's utmost rewards,
    first look into the content that is in you.

Another's Plan

I take notes, write, rewrite over and over,
    have instinct for selection,
discipline, give the work appealing form,
    convey sufficient meaning.
I like creating/ in fact I love it/ and
    I'm not in someone else's plan.

Hurrah For Imagination!

Frogs sometimes eat mice,
    not very nice,
why not just enjoy jumping,
    eye beautiful pond?
Brick becoming marble
    magician can't do,
but so what?
    Magic in everyone's story.
Castle of stone with glass wall surrounding
    wouldn't offer privacy,
but what delight
    for it to be polished and clear!
Trees don't have wings,
    but specialness is theirs,
speaking, listening, creating atmosphere,
    which many overlook.
Rocks don't wear mittens,
    but why should they?
They live a long time, and
    usually on firm ground.
So much of the planet stays absurd,
    what to do,
"cool head," courage, kindness,
    exercise, meditate,
think possibilities,
    sense a miracle.

The Attentive Poet

An attentive poet
writes one good poem a day
from his blessed,
sometimes mysterious, bubble,
perhaps
talks to flowers and weeds wisely,
sidewalk trees and minute cracks,
gentle rain that refreshes solitary pavement,
all delicate art for a hungry soul
that hopes to feel a new awakening
by his being astutely conscious
of fathering self.

The Sea

The sea, God's dream
    before the world was,
waves waving, speaking,
    mysterious deep.

Peace in its roar,
    free yet constrained,
difficult with ineffable beauty,
    wild but serene.

Says so much
    without words,
breathing greatness
    known to sailors and artists.

Where is Love?

Am I loved by a good book
    which teaches in a special way,
inspires happily, perhaps saying
    "Enjoy the learning."

Am I loved by a string of roses,
    pansies, violets, tulips, carnations,
delightful breathing art
    in tranquil garden?

Am I loved by friends who are gone?
    Do they watch careful steps,
outreaching hands, deep hurts, growing ways?
    Do they take in my feelings with caring eyes?

What IF

Had my path gone another way,
    who would be the relationships?
Would I see life's myths sooner?
    Would I have more right days?
Would I grasp earlier the power of study,
    exercise, nature, love?
Would I be less of a stranger
    to judging eyes?
Would I handle more skillfully
    the absurdities of life?
Would I grasp more deeply
    that the use of conscious power
is the measure of a person? *

Plato 427 B.C. - 347 B.C.
    *"The measure of a man is what he does
    with power."*
Abraham Lincoln 1809 - 1865
    *"If you want to test a man's character,
    give him power."*

Very Complex World

We are where we never thought we'd be,
    different selves,
different wellnesses,
    different feelings,
same heart.
    Many stories,
many missteps,
    many hopes,
few deep friends.
    No reason behind some things.
Mysteries in the sun. in the shadows.
    Evil, powerful,
but can't take your spirit
    unless you let it.
And how many lives
    have three halves?

Imagine

Imagine running up the world's highest mountain,
    only to find at the top
        three deeply-etched signs, all saying
            "It's the journey!"

Imagine stepping from a cloud,
        believing you'll touch down well,
            picturing and feeling a smooth landing
                before it happens!

Imagine having the right people around,
        who are truly gentle, caring souls,
            supporting each other
                in a conscious, cordial way!

Imagine gliding downhill on skis, balancing self
    in difficult grooves, wind on face,
        meditating on acceptance
            of where one is!

Windows

If walls could speak,
>would they be jealous of windows,

or a table that gets flowers,
>at times napkin, spoon, fork?

Would they mention unknown kindnesses,
>large ones, small ones,

those from great spirits
>that the world will not know?

Would they remain silent,
>just stare and glare,

as long as
>light is in the room?

Do windows feel?
>They see so much.

Education of a Soul

I've been a student of spirituality
    all my life,
but see myself
    at the beginnings of the art.
Awhile ago,
    I failed to look at the bright side,
my observing mind in slight confusion,
    ardent hope flickering,
thoughts saying,
    the years of study shaped an intellect,
    but what education to my soul?
Now to ask, what is my relationship to myself,
    to those who are in my life,
    to the outside world,
what steps reach my heart,
    how many touch my soul?

A Very Selfish Deed

They make their selfish decision.
The benefit comes,
but what a price for a soul!
Near the end before they go,
they ask, "Did I hurt you?"
You smile as if to say No.

A Very Simple Plan

To schedule tomorrow the night before,
so coming hours perhaps can soar.

Prioritize as best you can;
compose a practical plan.

It will lift your way
and help your day.

Order, the excellent key.
Who would disagree?

It inspires morning hello,
which can motivate "get up and go."

A simple step one can do!
Why so limited to a "few"?

Just Asking

WHEN subconscious speaks, will I hear glass-clear?

WHAT twists stories in their journey?

HOW is there magic in meditation?

WHY is life-long study transforming?

IF you believe in you, will the dream come true?

WILL we glimpse someday what is behind what we see?

DOES the isolated spirit always lose?

HOW MANY unmet loves are waiting?

A Poet...Yes!

He wanted to give crumbs to hungry minds,
     his training,
not having fulfilling job,
     empty feeling of abandonment,
hollow years of little emotional support,
     too much time alone,
hampering darkness in a world
     where others seem to have light,
relatively no family support for many years,
     mother afar a long time ago,
yet always there, as she is now,
     (though gravestone reads 50 years gone),
she who kept him going when thunder sounded,
     her kind, spirited, altruistic way
a memory and a model,
     and he, a continuation of her heart,
with plenty of room
     for his surrogate grandson...
all have converged to guide his ready pen.

Greatest Human Achievement

The future is about a goal and our soul,
      not where we are now or where we've been,
but being ever-conscious of the ***motivating phrase***
      meant for more light.

It's about "virtue mind," clean heart, uplifting spirit
      avoiding "stuckness" on homeward trail
of sharp pebbles, sudden turns, piercing shadows,
      soggy ground, falling trees, rolling rocks,

eyes forward, weighing within, striving continually
      to become the best possible person
by living each day as well as we can, sometimes
      with thin mist, low-lying fog, wandering steps.

$60,000

February 27, 2019

Anonymous gift of $60,000,
     small letter revealing,
a gift reward
     for life observed.

Tears came forth
     all that late afternoon,
early evening,
     next day too.

In a world which tends
     to be a bit mean
to some elders,
     kindness,
"the greatest wisdom," *
     has a great day.

* From the CD within the book,
Planting Seeds:Practicing
Mindfulness with Children
by Thich Nhat Hanh

ABOUT THE AUTHOR

CHARLES HOLMES writes to touch people's lives. He has written four life-reflecting poetry books, *For Understanding Eyes*, *Reflections of the Heart*, *Reflections of the Soul*, and *Streets That Speak*, that notes some realities of streets which do not have enough, and streets that do have enough. He also has compiled rich common sense in *Thoughts From Millie*, which is the result of many interviews when she was 89, 90, and 91 years old.

He has created three recreation centers for children, has taught at two universities and one community college, has done social work with the elderly poor, and has authored two studies about their difficulties.

He has delved into the magic of study formally and privately for many years.

He is a surrogate grandfather for an 11 year old boy named Aidan, grandson in heart.

Aidan Lee Elenteny, grandson in heart, and Charles Holmes

ACKNOWLEDGEMENTS

Joan Arnott

Barbara Elenteny

Sheila Helms

Michelle Lindner

Nadia McCaffrey

Rev. Bill McDonald

Nancy Montier

MeMe Riordan

To contact the author,
please email
rlg121212@gmail.com

67779742R00048

Made in the USA
Columbia, SC
01 August 2019